WITHDRAWN

WELCOME TO THE U.S.A.
TEXAS

Written by Ann Heinrichs   Illustrated by Matt Kania
Content Adviser: Stephen Cure, Director of Educational Services,
Texas State Historical Association, Austin, Texas

The Child's World

Published in the United States of America by The Child's World®
PO Box 326 • Chanhassen, MN 55317-0326
800-599-READ • www.childsworld.com

Photo Credits
Cover: Photodisc; frontispiece: Digital Vision.

Interior: Brand X Pictures: 10; Corbis: 6 (Left Lane Productions), 13 (Jan Butchofsky-Houser), 22 (Richard Cummins), 33 (Reuters); East Texas Oil Museum: 29; Library of Congress: 16; Buddy Mays/Corbis: 9, 14; Photodisc: 17; Picture Desk/Travelsite: 21 (Colasanti), 26 (Global); Poteet Strawberry Festival: 25; Thomas Rodman/Odessa Meteor Crater Museum: 34; Space Center Houston: 30; Walter Vasques/Charro Days: 18.

Acknowledgments
The Child's World®: Mary Berendes, Publishing Director

Editorial Directions, Inc.: E. Russell Primm, Editorial Director; Katie Marsico, Associate Editor; Judith Shiffer, Assistant Editor; Matt Messbarger, Editorial Assistant; Susan Hindman, Copy Editor; Melissa McDaniel, Proofreader; Kevin Cunningham, Peter Garnham, Matt Messbarger, Olivia Nellums, Chris Simms, Molly Symmonds, Katherine Trickle, Carl Stephen Wender, Fact Checkers; Tim Griffin/IndexServ, Indexer; Cian Loughlin O'Day, Photo Researcher and Editor

The Design Lab: Kathleen Petelinsek, Design; Julia Goozen, Art Production

Library of Congress Cataloging-in-Publication Data
Heinrichs, Ann.
    Texas / by Ann Heinrichs ; cartography and illustrations by Matt Kania.
        p. cm. — (Welcome to the U.S.A.)
    Includes index.
    ISBN 1-59296-485-0 (library bound : alk. paper) 1. Texas—Juvenile literature.
I. Kania, Matt, ill. II. Title. III. Series: Heinrichs, Ann. Welcome to the U.S.A.
F386.3.H453 2006
917.6404'64—dc22   2005002096

Ann Heinrichs is the author of more than 100 books for children and young adults. She has also enjoyed successful careers as a children's book editor and an advertising copywriter. Ann grew up in Fort Smith, Arkansas, and lives in Chicago, Illinois.

About the Author
Ann Heinrichs

Matt Kania loves maps and, as a kid, dreamed of making them. In school he studied geography and cartography, and today he makes maps for a living. Matt's favorite thing about drawing maps is learning about the places they represent. Many of the maps he has created can be found in books, magazines, videos, Web sites, and public places.

About the
Map Illustrator
Matt Kania

On the cover: Oil wells are a common site in Texas.
On page one: Big Bend National Park is popular with hikers.

OUR TEXAS TRIP

Welcome to Texas 4

Padre Island off the Gulf Coast 6

Wildlife in Big Bend National Park 9

Lubbock's Prairie Dogs 10

Ysleta del Sur Pueblo 13

San Antonio's Mission San José 14

Remember the Alamo! 17

Charro Days in Brownsville 18

A Cowboy Morning at the Elkins Ranch 21

The Texas State Fair in Dallas 22

The Poteet Strawberry Festival 25

The State Capitol in Austin 26

Kilgore's East Texas Oil Museum 29

Space Center Houston 30

The Bureau of Engraving and Printing in Fort Worth 33

Odessa's Meteor Crater 34

FOR MORE INFORMATION
Our Trip 37
Words to Know 37
State Symbols and Song 38
Famous People 39
To Find Out More 39
Index 40

Texas's Nickname:
The Lone Star State

Ready for a trip through the Lone Star State? That's Texas! It's a mighty big state. That means you're in for a mighty big adventure!

What will you do in Texas? You'll visit a community of prairie dogs. You'll gather seashells and climb sand dunes. You'll see what it's like to ride a space shuttle. You'll learn why Texans remember the Alamo. And you'll have a hearty breakfast with cowboys. Not bad for one state!

Are you ready? Then buckle up, and let's hit the road!

WELCOME TO
TEXAS

As you travel through Texas, watch for all the interesting facts along the way.

NEW MEXICO

OKLAHOMA

ARKANSAS

Amarillo 40

Red River 44

27

Lubbock

30

TEN

Fort Worth Dallas

LOUISIANA

Kilgore

20

El Paso

Odessa

TEXAS

Sabine River

10

Alpine

35

Austin

45

Houston

10

San Antonio

Rio Grande

Potpet

37

Padre Island

GULF OF MEXICO

MEXICO

Brownsville

Grab your shovel and pail! A boy builds a sandcastle on Padre Island.

Brownsville, Laredo, Del Rio, and El Paso are crossing points into Mexico.

Padre Island off the Gulf Coast

Tumble down a sand dune. Gather seashells on the beach. You're exploring Padre Island National Seashore!

Padre Island is long and narrow. It's called a barrier island. That's a long island just off a coast. It protects the coast from big waves.

Texas is a huge state. Only Alaska has a bigger land area. Southeastern Texas faces the Gulf of Mexico. The gulf is part of the Atlantic Ocean. Pine forests cover eastern Texas. Grassy plains stretch across much of the state. In the west are mountains and deserts.

The Rio Grande is one of Texas's major rivers. It forms the southern border with Mexico.

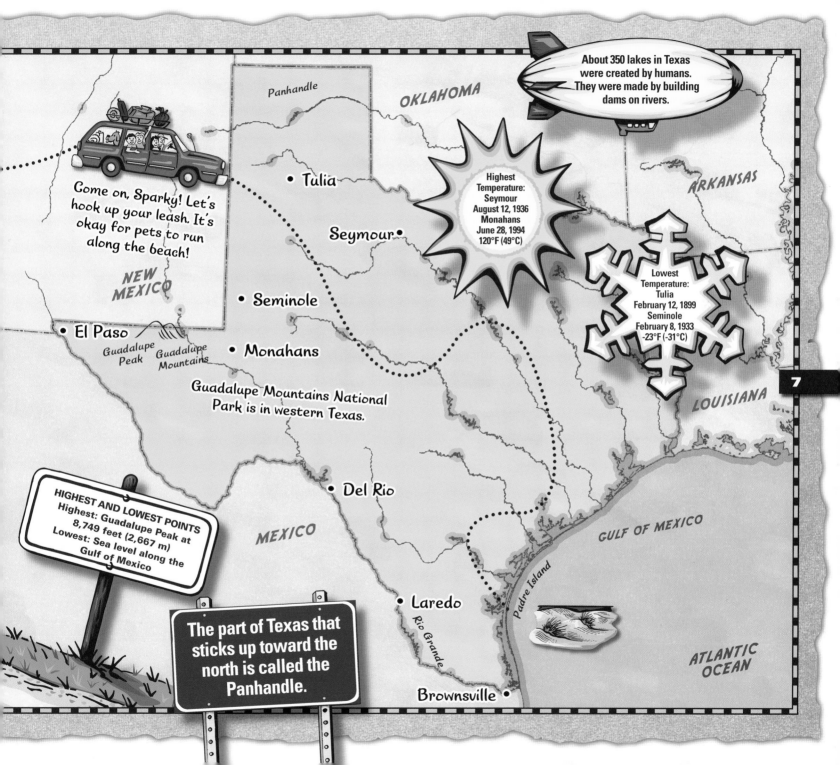

About 350 lakes in Texas were created by humans. They were made by building dams on rivers.

Panhandle

OKLAHOMA

ARKANSAS

Come on, Sparky! Let's hook up your leash. It's okay for pets to run along the beach!

NEW MEXICO

• Tulia

Seymour •

Highest Temperature:
Seymour
August 12, 1936
Monahans
June 28, 1994
120°F (49°C)

Lowest Temperature:
Tulia
February 12, 1899
Seminole
February 8, 1933
-23°F (-31°C)

• Seminole

• El Paso
Guadalupe Peak Guadalupe Mountains

• Monahans

LOUISIANA

Guadalupe Mountains National Park is in western Texas.

• Del Rio

HIGHEST AND LOWEST POINTS
Highest: Guadalupe Peak at 8,749 feet (2,667 m)
Lowest: Sea level along the Gulf of Mexico

MEXICO

GULF OF MEXICO

Padre Island

• Laredo
Rio Grande

The part of Texas that sticks up toward the north is called the Panhandle.

ATLANTIC OCEAN

Brownsville •

7

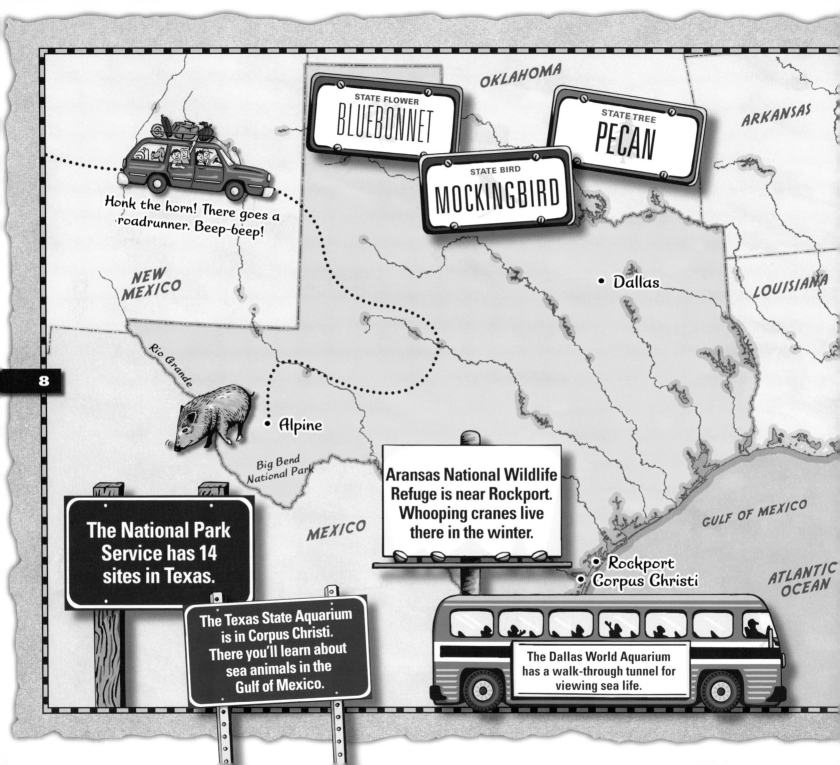

Honk the horn! There goes a roadrunner. Beep-beep!

STATE FLOWER
BLUEBONNET

STATE BIRD
MOCKINGBIRD

STATE TREE
PECAN

OKLAHOMA

ARKANSAS

NEW MEXICO

Rio Grande

Alpine

Big Bend National Park

MEXICO

• Dallas

LOUISIANA

GULF OF MEXICO

ATLANTIC OCEAN

Aransas National Wildlife Refuge is near Rockport. Whooping cranes live there in the winter.

• Rockport
• Corpus Christi

The National Park Service has 14 sites in Texas.

The Texas State Aquarium is in Corpus Christi. There you'll learn about sea animals in the Gulf of Mexico.

The Dallas World Aquarium has a walk-through tunnel for viewing sea life.

Wildlife in Big Bend National Park

Do you like seeing animals in the wild? Just roam around Big Bend National Park. It's along the Rio Grande south of Alpine. You'll see deer and coyotes. You might even spot mountain lions.

If you're camping out, prick up your ears. You may hear a snuffling sound at night. It could be a javelina looking for food. Javelinas are like wild pigs with bristly hair. Eek!

Lots of animals live off the coast. Sea turtles make their nests on the beaches. In the water, you'll see jellyfish and sharks.

This deer calls Big Bend National Park home.

Javelina comes from the Spanish word for "spear." That refers to the javelina's sharp tusks!

Not all owls live in trees. This one's home is an underground burrow in Lubbock!

Lubbock's Prairie Dogs

Head out to the east of Lubbock. You'll find a huge prairie dog town. Thousands of the furry little critters live there!

Prairie dogs are social animals. They always live in big communities. They dig long burrows, or tunnels, underground. That's where they live and raise their young.

Prairie dogs are related to squirrels and chipmunks. They often sit upright outside their holes. They make a barking sound when they're alarmed. That's how they got their name!

Burrowing owls live among the prairie dogs. The owls can't dig their own holes. They nest in the prairie dogs' burrows!

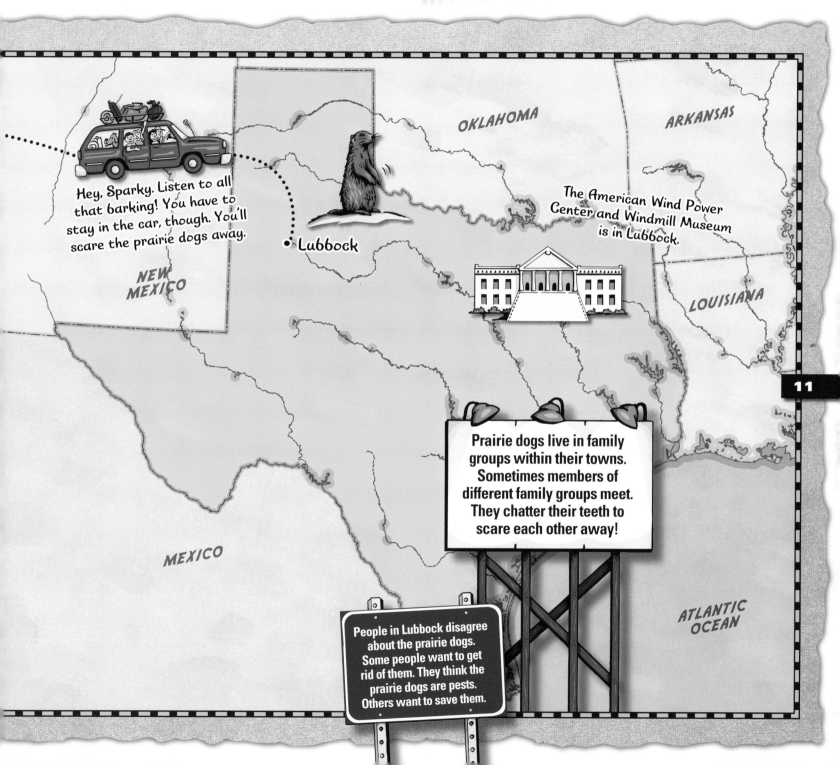

Hey, Sparky. Listen to all that barking! You have to stay in the car, though. You'll scare the prairie dogs away.

OKLAHOMA

ARKANSAS

The American Wind Power Center and Windmill Museum is in Lubbock.

• Lubbock

NEW MEXICO

LOUISIANA

Prairie dogs live in family groups within their towns. Sometimes members of different family groups meet. They chatter their teeth to scare each other away!

MEXICO

ATLANTIC OCEAN

People in Lubbock disagree about the prairie dogs. Some people want to get rid of them. They think the prairie dogs are pests. Others want to save them.

Yum! Smell that bread baking? We can eat some when it's nice and hot.

OKLAHOMA

ARKANSAS

Who Lived Here before Europeans Arrived? Atakapan, Caddo (Nacogdoches, Nasoni, Neche), Coahuiltecan, Jumano, Karankawa, Lipan Apache, Mescalero, Tonkawa, and Wichita

NEW MEXICO

LOUISIANA

• El Paso

• Alto

• Livingston

ATLANTIC OCEAN

MEXICO

Caddoan Mounds in Alto preserves an early Caddo settlement.

The name *Texas* comes from the Caddo Indian word *Tejas*, which means "friends."

Ysleta del Sur Pueblo

Watch how the people bake bread. They use a *horno*, or beehive-shaped oven. Then enjoy a lively dance show. Finally, you can join in a friendship dance.

You're visiting Ysleta del Sur **Pueblo.** It's a Tigua Indian community in El Paso.

Thousands of American Indians once lived in Texas. Some were farmers. Those along the coast caught fish and shellfish. Others hunted buffalo across the plains.

Spanish explorers arrived in the 1500s. Later, Spanish priests began opening **missions.** There they taught the Indians Christianity. Ysleta began as a Spanish mission. It's the oldest settlement in Texas. The Tigua have lived there since 1682.

Visitors tour a Tigua Indian pueblo.

The Alabama-Coushatta Indian Reservation is near Livingston.

Climb the winding steps of the church tower. Each step is carved from an oak log. See the building where grain was stored. It almost looks like a church, too.

You're visiting Mission San José. Missions were almost like small towns. They included vast fields and cattle herds. Indians did the farming and ranch work.

Mission San José opened in 1720. It was called the Queen of the Missions. About 300 Indians lived and worked there.

All this time, Texas was part of Spanish Mexico. Settlers began arriving from the United States. The first ones came in the early 1800s.

Don't forget to stop by Mission San José! You'll learn about Texas during the 1700s.

Mission San José's full name is Mission San José y San Miguel de Aguayo.

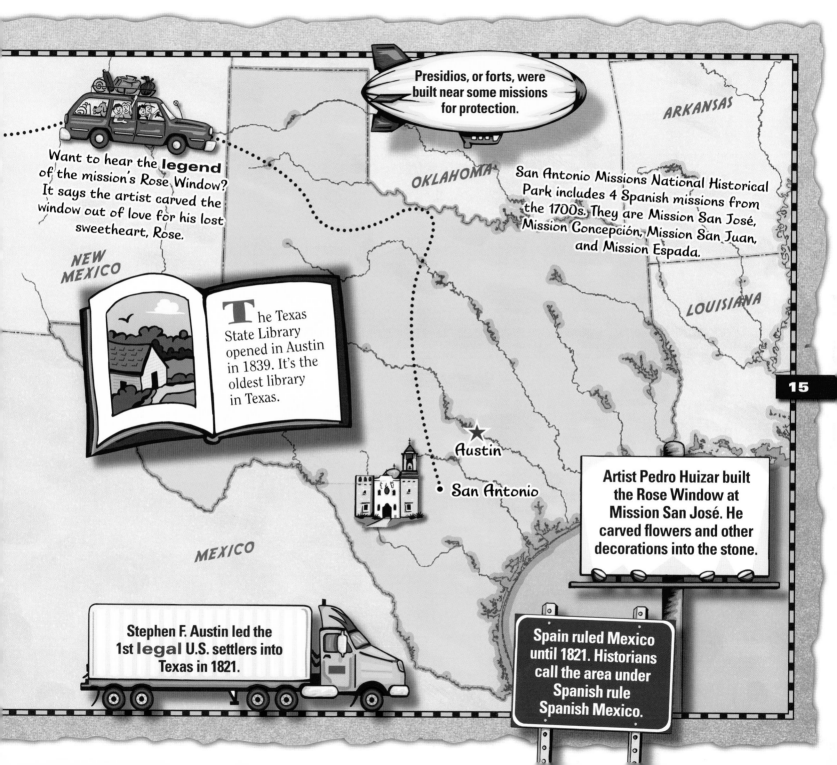

Presidios, or forts, were built near some missions for protection.

Want to hear the **legend** of the mission's Rose Window? It says the artist carved the window out of love for his lost sweetheart, Rose.

ARKANSAS

OKLAHOMA

San Antonio Missions National Historical Park includes 4 Spanish missions from the 1700s. They are Mission San José, Mission Concepción, Mission San Juan, and Mission Espada.

NEW MEXICO

LOUISIANA

The Texas State Library opened in Austin in 1839. It's the oldest library in Texas.

★ Austin

San Antonio

Artist Pedro Huizar built the Rose Window at Mission San José. He carved flowers and other decorations into the stone.

MEXICO

Stephen F. Austin led the 1st legal U.S. settlers into Texas in 1821.

Spain ruled Mexico until 1821. Historians call the area under Spanish rule Spanish Mexico.

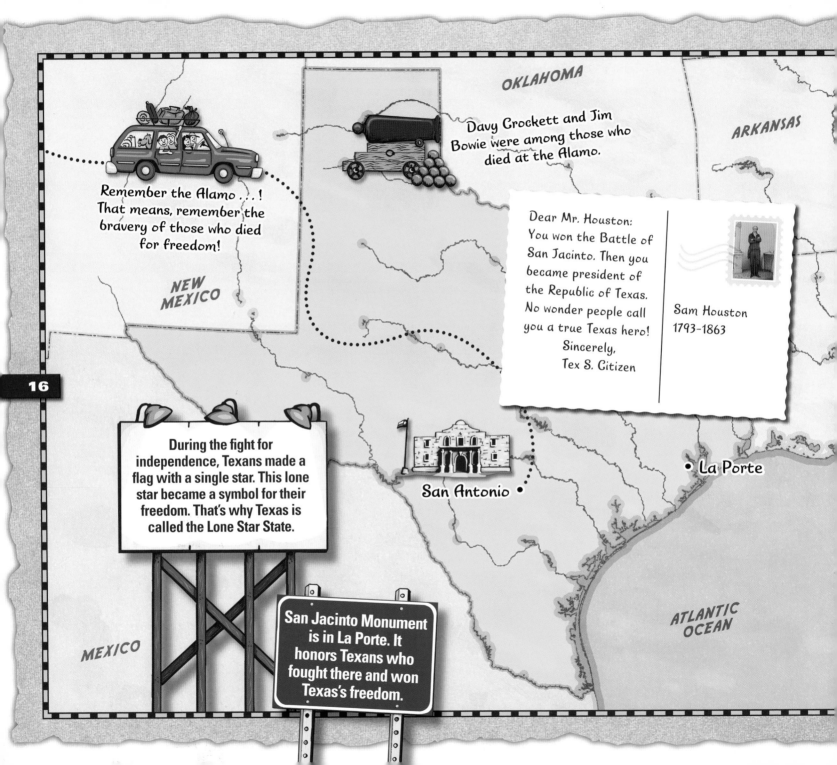

Remember the Alamo . . . ! That means, remember the bravery of those who died for freedom!

NEW MEXICO

OKLAHOMA

ARKANSAS

Davy Crockett and Jim Bowie were among those who died at the Alamo.

Dear Mr. Houston:
You won the Battle of San Jacinto. Then you became president of the Republic of Texas. No wonder people call you a true Texas hero!
Sincerely,
Tex S. Citizen

Sam Houston
1793–1863

During the fight for independence, Texans made a flag with a single star. This lone star became a symbol for their freedom. That's why Texas is called the Lone Star State.

San Antonio

La Porte

MEXICO

San Jacinto Monument is in La Porte. It honors Texans who fought there and won Texas's freedom.

ATLANTIC OCEAN

Remember the Alamo!

Be sure to visit the Alamo in San Antonio! A fierce battle took place there in 1836. Many Texans wanted freedom from Mexico. They fought the Texas Revolution. Freedom fighters were defending the Alamo. More than 180 people fought and died there. Then Texans wanted freedom even more. Their battle cry was "Remember the Alamo!"

Sam Houston led the final battle against Mexico. It was the Battle of San Jacinto. Then Texas became an independent country. It was called the Republic of Texas.

Texas was an independent republic from 1836 to 1845.

Want to know more about Texas's fight for independence? Just visit the Alamo in San Antonio.

The Alamo was both a fort and a mission. It began in 1718 as Mission San Antonio de Valero.

Charro Days features colorful costumes and exciting parades.

A *charro* is a gallant Mexican horseman. The charro suit is a traditional Mexican costume.

Charro Days in Brownsville

Girls and women wear ruffly dresses. Boys and men wear sombreros. Those are big Mexican hats. Everyone's costumes are brilliantly decorated. It's time for Charro Days!

Charro Days is a big Mexican American festival. People in Matamoras, Mexico, join in, too. That city is right across the border.

Almost one out of three Texans is Hispanic. They are people with roots in Spanish-speaking lands. They hold fiestas, or festivals, throughout the year.

Delicious spicy foods are part of every fiesta. Mexican foods are popular in Texas. They include tacos, chili peppers, and **enchiladas.** Many Texans blend Mexican and U.S. food **traditions.** The result? Tex-Mex food!

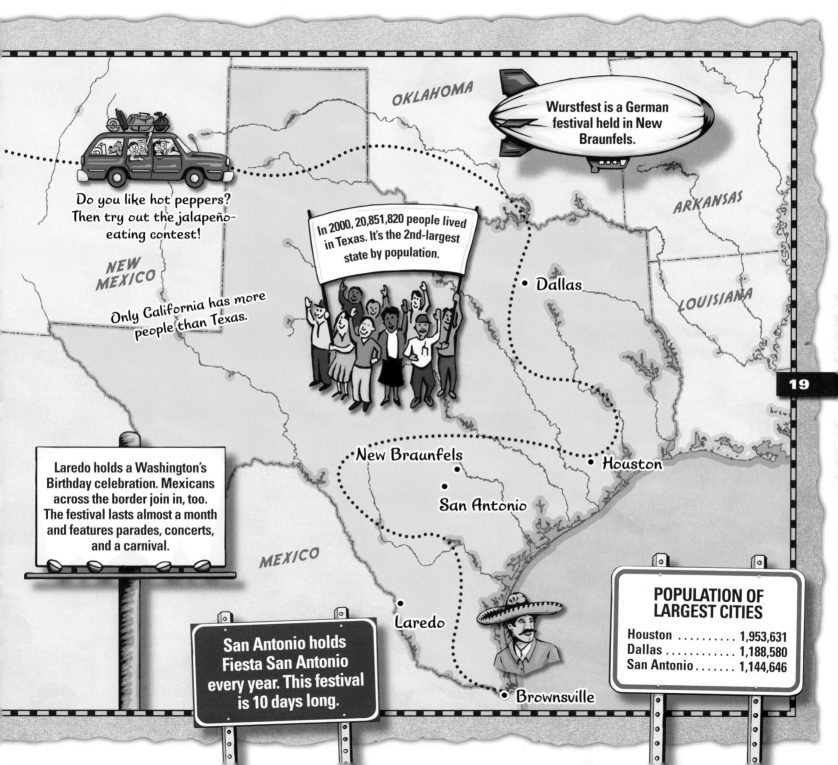

OKLAHOMA

Wurstfest is a German festival held in New Braunfels.

ARKANSAS

Do you like hot peppers? Then try out the jalapeño-eating contest!

NEW MEXICO

In 2000, 20,851,820 people lived in Texas. It's the 2nd-largest state by population.

Only California has more people than Texas.

LOUISIANA

• Dallas

19

Laredo holds a Washington's Birthday celebration. Mexicans across the border join in, too. The festival lasts almost a month and features parades, concerts, and a carnival.

New Braunfels •

• Houston

• San Antonio

MEXICO

San Antonio holds Fiesta San Antonio every year. This festival is 10 days long.

• Laredo

POPULATION OF LARGEST CITIES

Houston 1,953,631
Dallas 1,188,580
San Antonio 1,144,646

• Brownsville

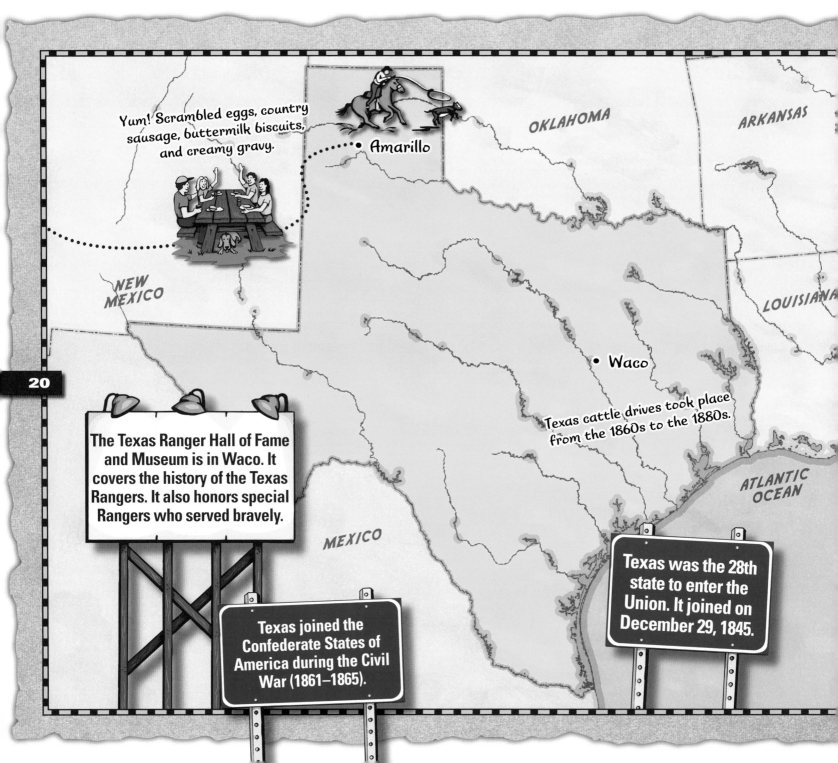

Yum! Scrambled eggs, country sausage, buttermilk biscuits, and creamy gravy.

OKLAHOMA

ARKANSAS

Amarillo

NEW MEXICO

LOUISIANA

Waco

Texas cattle drives took place from the 1860s to the 1880s.

The Texas Ranger Hall of Fame and Museum is in Waco. It covers the history of the Texas Rangers. It also honors special Rangers who served bravely.

MEXICO

ATLANTIC OCEAN

Texas was the 28th state to enter the Union. It joined on December 29, 1845.

Texas joined the Confederate States of America during the Civil War (1861–1865).

The Elkins Ranch overlooks Palo Duro Canyon.

Climb aboard a jeep with horns on the front. Then ride out across the range. The cook rustles up a breakfast. Then cowboys put on a show. You're having a Cowboy Morning! It's at the Elkins Ranch near Amarillo.

Cowboys are a big part of Texas **culture.** Many new settlers in Texas started cattle ranches. They hired cowboys to do the ranch work.

The Texas Rangers were officially organized in 1835. These horseback lawmen kept peace and protected settlers. Texas Rangers still keep peace in Texas today!

Ride, 'em, cowboy—or cowgirl! Cowboys play an important role in Texas's history and culture.

Want to dance? These performers are at the Texas State Fair in Dallas.

The Dallas Burn soccer team changed its name to FC Dallas in 2005.

The Texas State Fair in Dallas

Animal shows, cattle barns, concerts, and yummy food. Where can you find these all in one place? At the Texas State Fair! It's held every October in Dallas's Fair Park.

The state fair is Texas's biggest event. About 3 million people attend every year. And it lasts more than three weeks!

Rodeos are popular events in Texas, too. People come to show off their cowboy skills. They ride bucking horses and rope cattle.

Cowboys are an important part of life in Texas. Many Texans dress like cowboys and cowgirls. They wear boots, cowboy hats, and big belt buckles!

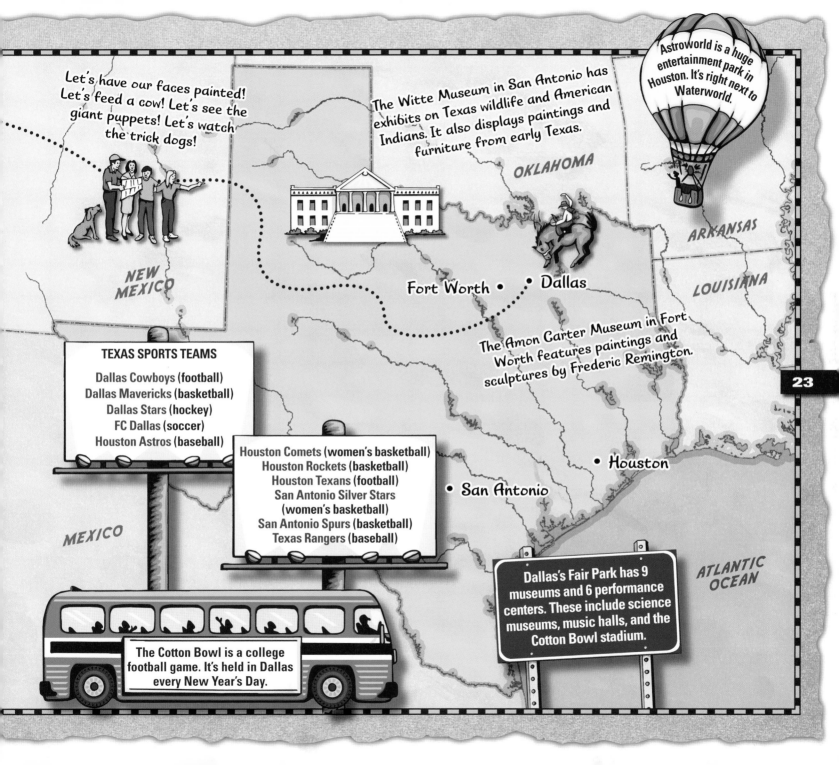

Let's have our faces painted! Let's feed a cow! Let's see the giant puppets! Let's watch the trick dogs!

The Witte Museum in San Antonio has exhibits on Texas wildlife and American Indians. It also displays paintings and furniture from early Texas.

Astroworld is a huge entertainment park in Houston. It's right next to Waterworld.

OKLAHOMA

NEW MEXICO

ARKANSAS

LOUISIANA

Fort Worth •   • Dallas

The Amon Carter Museum in Fort Worth features paintings and sculptures by Frederic Remington.

TEXAS SPORTS TEAMS

Dallas Cowboys (football)
Dallas Mavericks (basketball)
Dallas Stars (hockey)
FC Dallas (soccer)
Houston Astros (baseball)

Houston Comets (women's basketball)
Houston Rockets (basketball)
Houston Texans (football)
San Antonio Silver Stars (women's basketball)
San Antonio Spurs (basketball)
Texas Rangers (baseball)

• Houston

• San Antonio

MEXICO

ATLANTIC OCEAN

Dallas's Fair Park has 9 museums and 6 performance centers. These include science museums, music halls, and the Cotton Bowl stadium.

The Cotton Bowl is a college football game. It's held in Dallas every New Year's Day.

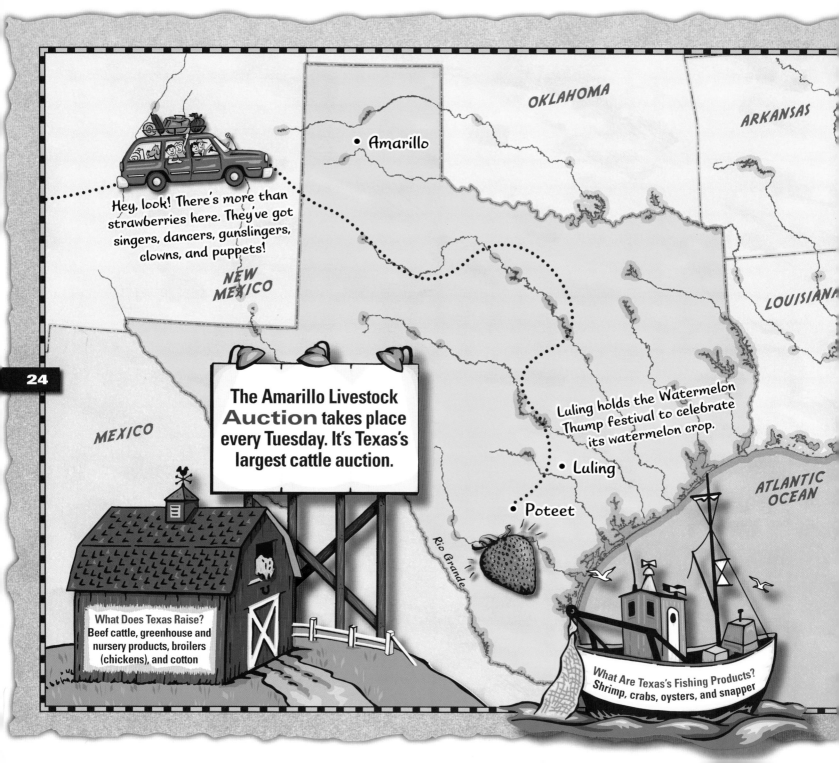

OKLAHOMA

ARKANSAS

• Amarillo

Hey, look! There's more than strawberries here. They've got singers, dancers, gunslingers, clowns, and puppets!

NEW MEXICO

LOUISIANA

The Amarillo Livestock **Auction** takes place every Tuesday. It's Texas's largest cattle auction.

MEXICO

Luling holds the Watermelon Thump festival to celebrate its watermelon crop.

• Luling

ATLANTIC OCEAN

• Poteet

Rio Grande

What Does Texas Raise? Beef cattle, greenhouse and nursery products, broilers (chickens), and cotton

What Are Texas's Fishing Products? Shrimp, crabs, oysters, and snapper

The Poteet Strawberry Festival

It's the king and queen of Poteet's Strawberry Festival! This tasty event features games and contests.

Strawberries dipped in chocolate. Strawberries swimming in whipped cream. Strawberries piled high on cakes. Does this sound like your kind of fun? Then head for the Poteet Strawberry Festival!

This festival celebrates a delicious Texas crop. But cotton is the top crop. No other state grows more cotton than Texas.

The Rio Grande valley has a warm climate. Farmers there grow many crops. They can even grow crops in the winter.

Texas has more farmland than any other state. Much of that land belongs to cattle ranches. Beef cattle graze across vast stretches of grassland. Texas cowboys are as busy as ever today. They rope, brand, and round up cattle.

Texas lawmakers work inside the capitol in Austin.

The State Capitol in Austin

Texans like to say everything's bigger in Texas. When you see the capitol, you'll agree. It's the biggest state capitol in the country. It's taller than the U.S. Capitol in Washington, D.C.

Many state government offices are in the capitol. There are three branches of government. One makes the laws. Another branch carries out the laws. It's headed by the governor. The third branch is made up of judges. They study the law. Then they apply it in courts. They decide if someone has broken the law.

Texas's capitol was built out of pink granite. That granite filled 15,000 railroad cars!

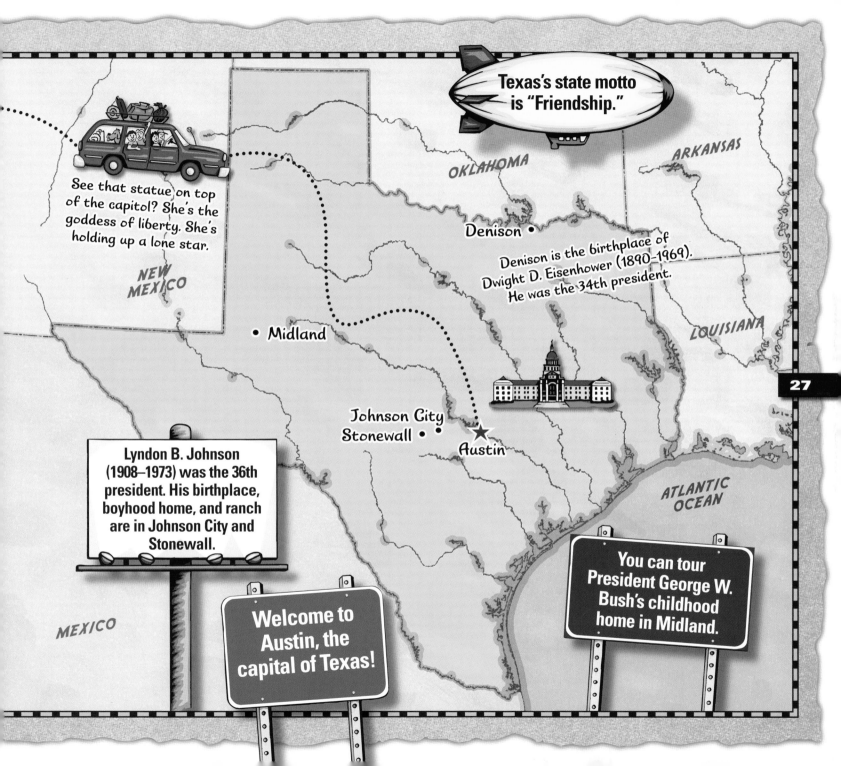

Texas's state motto is "Friendship."

See that statue on top of the capitol? She's the goddess of liberty. She's holding up a lone star.

Denison is the birthplace of Dwight D. Eisenhower (1890–1969). He was the 34th president.

Lyndon B. Johnson (1908–1973) was the 36th president. His birthplace, boyhood home, and ranch are in Johnson City and Stonewall.

Welcome to Austin, the capital of Texas!

You can tour President George W. Bush's childhood home in Midland.

27

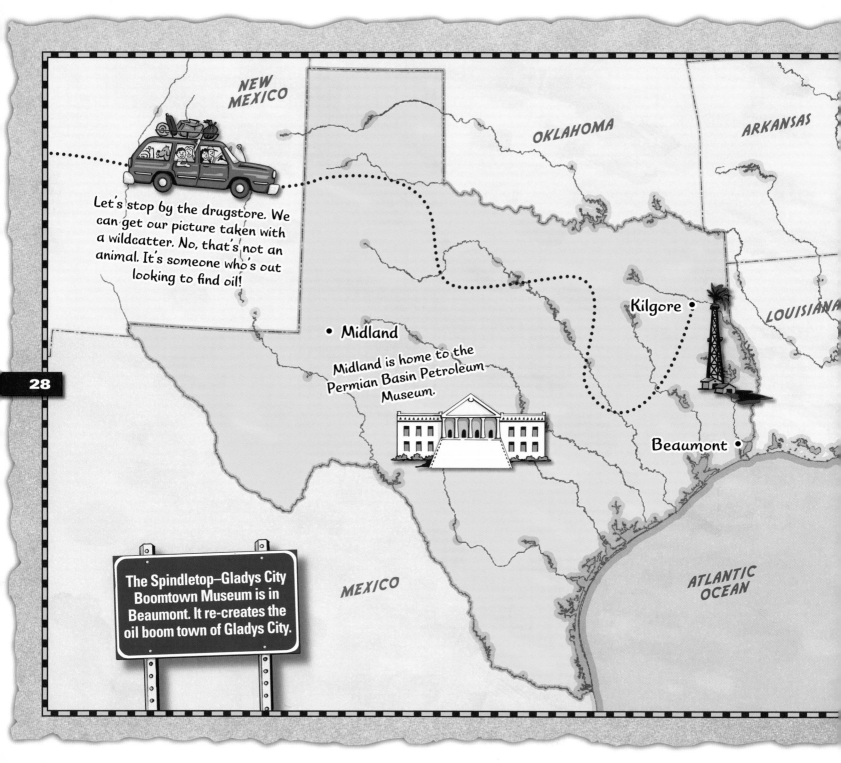

NEW MEXICO

OKLAHOMA

ARKANSAS

LOUISIANA

Let's stop by the drugstore. We can get our picture taken with a wildcatter. No, that's not an animal. It's someone who's out looking to find oil!

Kilgore

• Midland

Midland is home to the Permian Basin Petroleum Museum.

Beaumont •

MEXICO

ATLANTIC OCEAN

The Spindletop–Gladys City Boomtown Museum is in Beaumont. It re-creates the oil boom town of Gladys City.

Fill it up! Young visitors tour an exhibit at the East Texas Oil Museum.

Walk the streets of an oil **boom town.** Pump your own gas at the gas station. Ride an elevator deep into the Earth. There you'll see where oil deposits lie.

You're exploring the East Texas Oil Museum! It brings the oil boom days to life.

The Spindletop oil well opened in 1901. It was near Beaumont, on the Gulf Coast. Suddenly, oil became a booming **industry.** Many **oil fields** contained natural gas, too.

People kept finding more oil around the state. The biggest discovery was the East Texas oil field. It was found near Kilgore in 1930.

29

Is this how astronauts train at Space Center Houston? Kids play in the Martian Matrix exhibit.

The *Apollo 11* astronauts were Edwin (Buzz) Aldrin, Neil Armstrong, and Michael Collins.

Space Center Houston

op on a Moon **rover.** Pilot a space shuttle. See what a space voyage is like. You're visiting Space Center Houston! It's part of Johnson Space Center. That's where astronauts are trained.

Texas grew fast in the 1900s. Oil was just one of its booming industries. Another big business was the space industry.

Johnson Space Center began as the Manned Spacecraft Center. It opened in 1964. It directed space flights that had humans aboard. The center took a big step in 1969. It sent *Apollo 11* into space. Its astronauts were the first people on the Moon!

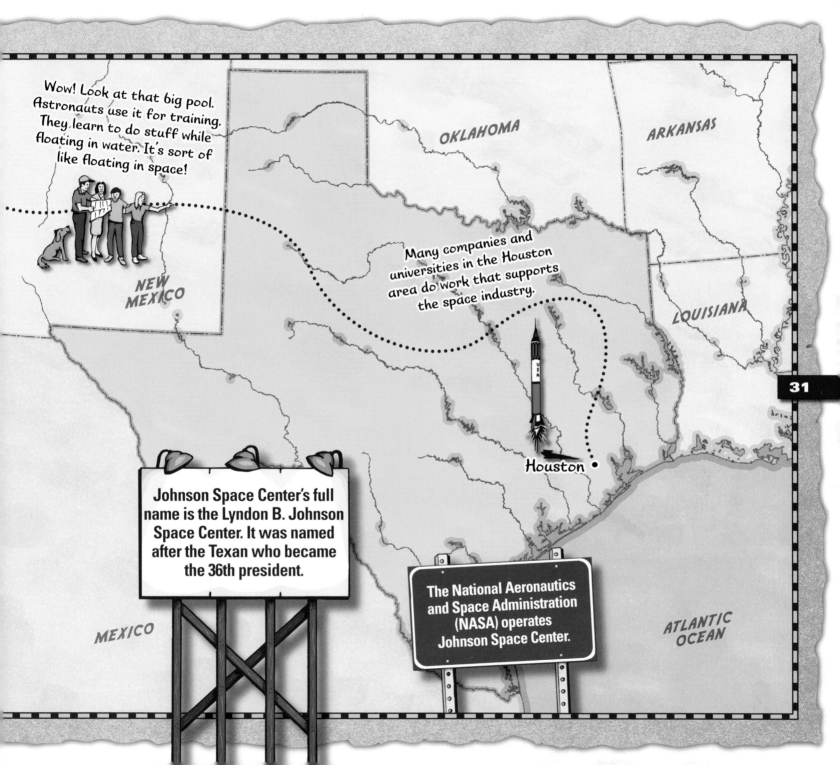

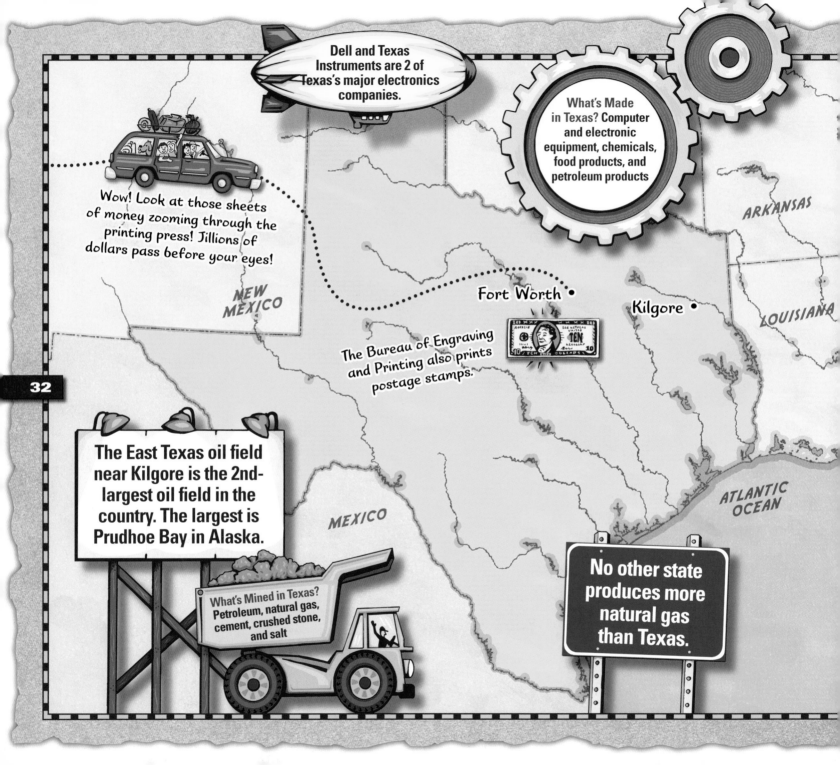

The Bureau of Engraving and Printing in Fort Worth

Want to tour a money factory? Just visit the Bureau of Engraving and Printing. Its Western Currency Facility is in Fort Worth. It prints paper money for the U.S. government. You'll see billions of dollars being printed there!

The money factory is pretty exciting. But Texas factories make lots more than money. Computers and other electronics are the leading products. Chemicals are important, too. Texas makes many oil-related chemicals.

Speaking of oil, let's not forget mining. Texas is the number-one mining state. That's because Texas mines so much oil and gas.

Does this job pay well? A worker examines bills at the Bureau of Engraving and Printing.

The Bureau of Engraving and Printing has 2 locations. One is in Fort Worth. The other is in Washington, D.C.

Odessa's Meteor Crater

A visitor studies meteors at Odessa's museum.

34

The Odessa meteor crater measures about 550 feet (168 m) across.

Pow! The **meteor** crashes with a deafening thud. Earth trembles and shakes. Dust clouds swirl up and fill the sky.

Luckily, you're not watching this. You might not have survived! It happened about 25,000 years ago. Now all that's left is the meteor's crater. It's a big, bowl-shaped hole near Odessa.

You won't see the meteor itself. It broke apart when it landed. Hundreds of meteor pieces have been found nearby.

Check out the museum at the crater site. You'll learn all about the Odessa meteor. You'll also learn about other materials from space. When night comes, you'll find yourself looking up!

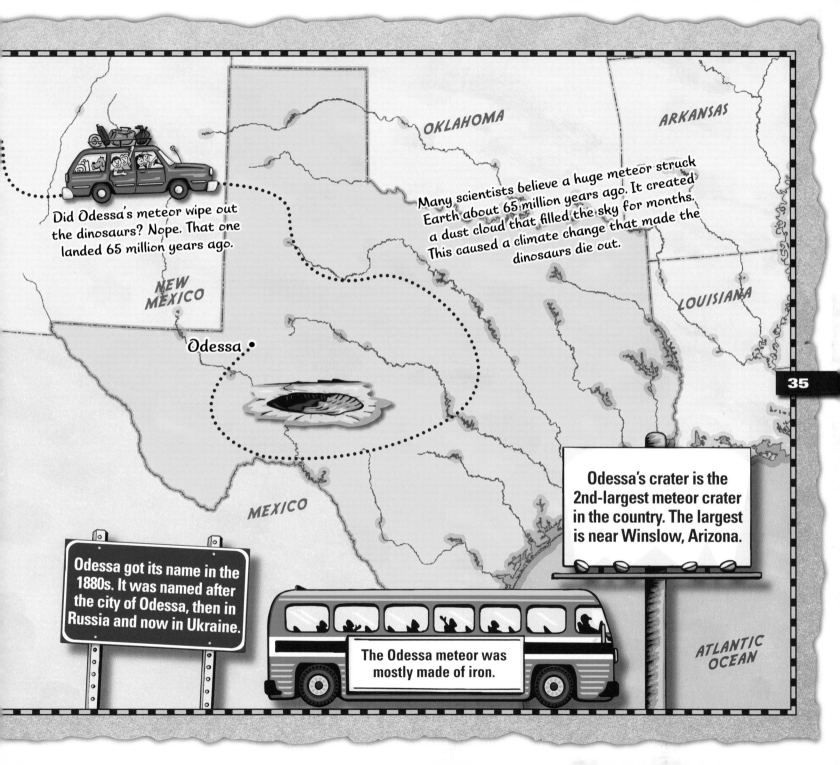

Did Odessa's meteor wipe out the dinosaurs? Nope. That one landed 65 million years ago.

Many scientists believe a huge meteor struck Earth about 65 million years ago. It created a dust cloud that filled the sky for months. This caused a climate change that made the dinosaurs die out.

OKLAHOMA

ARKANSAS

NEW MEXICO

Odessa •

LOUISIANA

MEXICO

ATLANTIC OCEAN

Odessa's crater is the 2nd-largest meteor crater in the country. The largest is near Winslow, Arizona.

Odessa got its name in the 1880s. It was named after the city of Odessa, then in Russia and now in Ukraine.

The Odessa meteor was mostly made of iron.

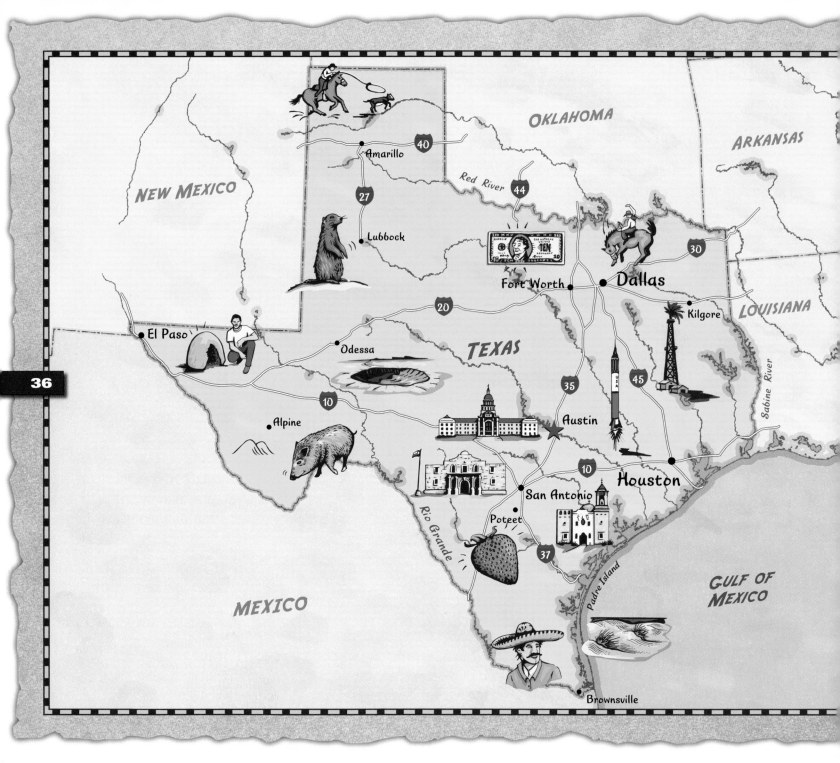

OKLAHOMA

ARKANSAS

NEW MEXICO

Red River

Amarillo 40

27

44

Lubbock

30

Fort Worth

Dallas

LOUISIANA

Kilgore

20

El Paso

Odessa

TEXAS

Sabine River

Alpine

35

45

Austin

10

Houston

San Antonio

Rio Grande

Poteet

37

MEXICO

Padre Island

GULF OF MEXICO

Brownsville

OUR TRIP

We visited many amazing places on our trip! We also met a lot of interesting people along the way. Look at the map on the left. Use your finger to trace all the places we have been.

How many human-made lakes does Texas have? See page 7 for the answer.

Where is the Texas State Aquarium located? Page 8 has the answer.

Who led the first legal settlers into Texas? See page 15 for the answer.

What is a charro? Look on page 18 for the answer.

What side did Texas join during the Civil War? Page 20 has the answer.

When and where is the Cotton Bowl held? Turn to page 23 for the answer.

What is Texas's largest cattle auction? Look on page 24 to find out!

Who were the *Apollo 11* astronauts? Turn to page 30 for the answer.

That was a great trip! We have traveled all over Texas!

There are a few places that we didn't have time for, though. Next time, we plan to visit the Congress Avenue Bridge in Austin. It's also known as the Bat Bridge. Visitors gather there from March through September. Every night, they watch 1.5 million Mexican free-tailed bats come out to hunt mosquitos.

More Places to Visit in Texas

WORDS TO KNOW

auction (AWK-shuhn) a sale where people bid or offer money for something

boom town (BOOM TOUN) a town that grew up quickly because of a new business

culture (KUHL-chur) a group of people's special customs, beliefs, and way of life

enchiladas (en-chuh-LA-duhz) tortillas wrapped around a filling and covered with sauce

industry (IN-duh-stree) a type of business

legal (LEE-guhl) allowed by the law

legend (LEJ-uhnd) a story told from long ago

meteor (MEE-tee-ur) pieces of rock or other material from space that come close to Earth

missions (MISH-uhnz) centers set up for spreading a faith

oil fields (OIL FEELDZ) regions where oil lies underground

pueblo (PWEB-loh) an American Indian village

reservation (rez-ur-VAY-shuhn) land set aside for a special use, such as for Native Americans

rover (ROH-vur) a vehicle that travels across land to gather information

traditions (truh-DISH-uhnz) customs passed down over many years

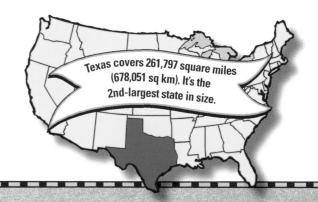

Texas covers 261,797 square miles (678,051 sq km). It's the 2nd-largest state in size.

STATE SYMBOLS

State bird: Mockingbird

State dish: Chili

State fiber and fabric: Cotton

State fish: Guadalupe bass

State flower: Bluebonnet

State flying mammal: Mexican free-tailed bat

State folk dance: Square dance

State fruit: Texas red grapefruit

State gem: Texas blue topaz

State grass: Sideoats grama

State insect: Monarch butterfly

State large mammal: Longhorn

State pepper: Jalapeño

State plant: Prickly pear cactus

State reptile: Horned lizard

State shell: Lightning whelk

State shrub: Crape myrtle

State small mammal: Armadillo

State sport: Rodeo

State tree: Pecan

State vegetable: Sweet onion

State flag   State seal

STATE SONG

"Texas, Our Texas"

Words by William J. Marsh and Gladys Yoakum Wright;

music by William J. Marsh

Texas, our Texas! All hail the mighty State!
Texas, our Texas! So wonderful, so great!
Boldest and grandest, withstanding ev'ry test;
O Empire wide and glorious, You stand supremely blest.

Chorus:
God bless you Texas! And keep you brave and strong,
That you may grow in power and worth, Thro'out the ages long.

Texas, O Texas! Your freeborn single star,
Sends out its radiance to nations near and far.
Emblem of freedom! It sets our hearts aglow,
With thoughts of San Jacinto and glorious Alamo.

(Chorus)

Texas, dear Texas! From tyrant grip now free,
Shines forth in splendor your star of destiny!
Mother of heroes! We come your children true,
Proclaiming our allegiance, our faith, our love for you.

(Chorus)

FAMOUS PEOPLE

Ailey, Alvin (1931–1989), dancer and choreographer

Armstrong, Lance (1971–), cyclist

Austin, Stephen F. (1793–1836), American pioneer who brought U.S. settlers to Texas

Austin, Steve (1964–), wrestler

Bond, Felicia (1952–), children's book author and illustrator

Burnett, Carol (1933–), actor and comedian

Bush, George W. (1946–), 43rd U.S. president

Cronkite, Walter (1916–), journalist and television newscaster

Eisenhower, Dwight D. (1890–1969), 34th U.S. president

Foreman, George (1949–), boxer

Holly, Buddy (1936–1959), rock 'n' roll musician

Houston, Samuel (1793–1863), soldier and politician

Johnson, Lyndon B. (1908–1973), 36th U.S. president

Johnson, Michael (1967–), track star and Olympic gold medalist

Joplin, Scott (1868–1917), composer and pianist

Marshall, James (1942–1992), children's author and illustrator

Parker, Quanah (ca. 1845–1911), leader of the Comanche Indians

Perez, Selena Quintanilla (1971–1995), singer

Petty, Richard (1937–), NASCAR driver

Roddenberry, Gene (1921–1991), creator of *Star Trek*

Ryan, Nolan (1947–), baseball *Hall of Fame* pitcher

TO FIND OUT MORE

At the Library
Burgan, Michael. *George W. Bush: Our Forty-Third President.* Chanhassen, Minn.: The Child's World, 2005.

Casad, Mary Brooke, and Benjamin Vincent (illustrator). *Bluebonnet at the Texas State Capitol.* Grenta, La.: Pelican Pub., 1997.

Crane, Carol, and Alan Stacy (illustrator). *L Is for Lone Star: A Texas Alphabet.* Chelsea, Mich.: Sleeping Bear Press, 2001.

Gurasich, Marj. *Did You Ever—Meet a Texas Hero?* Austin, Tex.: Eakin Press, 1992.

Hopkins, Jackie, and Kay Salem (illustrator). *Tumbleweed Tom on the Texas Trail.* Watertown, Mass.: Charlesbridge, 1994.

On the Web
Visit our home page for lots of links about Texas:
http://www.childsworld.com/links

Note to Parents, Teachers, and Librarians: We routinely verify our Web links to make sure they are safe, active sites—so encourage your readers to check them out!

Places to Visit or Contact
The Bob Bullock Texas State History Museum
1800 North Congress Avenue
Austin, TX 78701
512/936-8746
For more information about the history of Texas

Office of the Governor, Economic Development & Tourism
1700 North Congress Avenue, Suite 200
Austin, TX 78701
512/936-0101
For more information about traveling in Texas

INDEX

Alabama-Coushatta Indian Reservation, 13
Alamo, 17, 17
Aldrin, Edwin "Buzz," 30
Alpine, 9
Alto, 12
Amarillo Livestock Auction, 24
American Indians, 12, 13, 14
animals, 8, 9, 9, 10, 10, 11
Apollo 11 spacecraft, 30
Aransas National Wildlife Refuge, 8
Armstrong, Neil, 30
Atlantic Ocean, 6
Austin, 26, 27

barrier islands, 6
Battle of San Jacinto, 17
Beaumont, 28, 29
Big Bend National Park, 9, 9
bluebonnet (state flower), 8
boom towns, 28, 29
borders, 6
Brownsville, 6, 18
Bureau of Engraving and Printing, 33
burrowing owls, 10, 10
Bush, George W., 27

Caddo Indians, 12
Caddoan Mounds, 12
cattle auctions, 24
cattle drives, 21
Charro Days, 18, 18
charros, 18
Civil War, 20
climate, 7, 25
coastline, 9, 13
Collins, Michael, 30

Confederate States of America, 20
Corpus Christi, 8
cotton, 25
Cotton Bowl stadium, 23
Cowboy Morning, 21
cowboys, 21, 21, 22, 25
cowgirls, 21, 22
craters, 34, 35

Dallas, 19, 22
Dallas Burn soccer team, 22
Del Rio, 6

East Texas oil field, 29, 32
East Texas Oil Museum, 29, 29
El Paso, 6, 13
elevation, 7
Elkins Ranch, 21

Fair Park, 23
farming, 13, 14, 21, 24, 25
FC Dallas soccer team, 22, 23
Fiesta San Antonio, 19
fiestas, 18
foods, 18
Fort Worth, 33

Gladys City, 28
governors, 26
Guadalupe Peak, 7
Gulf Coast, 29
Gulf of Mexico, 6, 7

Hispanics, 18
Houston, 19, 30
Houston, Sam, 16, 16
Huizar, Pedro, 15

industries, 29, 30, 32, 33

javelinas, 9
Johnson City, 27
Johnson, Lyndon B., 27, 31
Johnson Space Center, 30, 31
judges, 26

Kilgore, 29, 32

landforms, 6, 7, 9, 12, 13, 34, 35
landmarks, 17, 17, 26, 26, 34 ,35
LaPorte, 16
Laredo, 6, 19
livestock, 21, 24, 25
Livingston, 13
Lubbock, 10, 11

major cities, 6, 13, 17, 19, 22, 26, 27, 30, 33
Manned Spacecraft Center, 30
marine life, 9, 13
Matamoras, Mexico, 18
Meteor Crater Museum, 34, 34
meteors, 34, 35
Midland, 27
mining, 29, 30, 33
Mission San Antonio de Valero, 17
Mission San José, 14, 14, 15
missions, 13, 14
mockingbird (state bird), 8

National Aeronautics and Space Administration

(NASA), 31
national parks, 8, 9, 9
natural gas, 29, 32
natural resources, 32, 33

Odessa, 34, 35
oil industry, 29, 30, 32, 33

Padre Island, 6, 6
Padre Island National Seashore, 6
Panhandle, 7
pecan (state tree), 8
places of interest, 6, 6, 8, 12, 13, 13, 14, 14, 15, 16, 17, 17, 20, 21, 21, 23, 26, 26, 27, 28, 29, 29, 30, 30, 31, 33, 33, 34, 34
plants, 6, 8
population, 19
Poteet Strawberry Festival, 25, 25
prairie dogs, 10, 11

Queen of the Missions, 14

ranches, 21, 25
Republic of Texas, 16, 17
Rio Grande, 6, 9, 25
Rockport, 8
rodeos, 22
Rose Window, 15

San Antonio, 17, 19
San Jacinto Monument, 16
settlers, 14, 21
Space Center Houston, 30, 30
space industry, 30, 31

Spanish exploration, 13
Spanish Mexico, 14, 15
Spindletop oil well, 29
Spindletop-Gladys City Boomtown Museum, 28
sports, 22, 23
state bird, 8
state capital, 27
state capitol, 26, 26
state flower, 8
state government, 26
state nickname, 4, 16
state tree, 8
statehood, 20
Stonewall, 27

Tex-Mex food, 18
Texas Ranger Hall of Fame and Museum, 20
Texas Rangers, 20, 21
Texas Revolution, 16, 17
Texas State Aquarium, 8
Texas State Fair, 22, 22
Tigua Indians, 13

Waco, 20
Washington's Birthday celebrations, 19
Western Currency Facility, 33

Ysleta, 13
Ysleta del Sur Pueblo, 13, 13

Bye, Lone Star State. We had a great time. We'll come back soon!